W9-BLR-579

R02084 57075

DISCARD

DATE DUE

OCT 2 4 2005			
NOV 1 0 2005			

DEMCO 38-296

THE CHICAGO PUBLIC LIBRARY

DISCARD

ORIOLE PARK BRANCH
7454 W. BALMORAL
CHICAGO, IL 60656

SCIENCE PROJECT IDEAS

Science Project Ideas About

AIR

Robert Gardner

Enslow Publishers, Inc.

40 Industrial Road   PO Box 38
Box 398   Aldershot
Berkeley Heights, NJ 07922   Hants GU12 6BP
USA   UK
http://www.enslow.com

Copyright © 1997 by Robert Gardner

All rights reserved.

No part of this book may be reproduced by any means
without the written permission of the publisher.

Library of Congress Cataloging-in-Publication Data

Gardner, Robert, 1929–
    Science project ideas about air / Robert Gardner.
        p. cm.—(Science project ideas)
    Includes bibliographical references and index.
    Summary: Presents experiments that reveal the properties of air, with
special attention to those that would make good science fair projects.
    ISBN 0-89490-838-3
    1. Air—Experiments—Juvenile literature. 2. Science projects—Juvenile
literature. [1. Air—Experiments. 2. Experiments. 3. Science projects.]
I. Title. II. Series: Gardner, Robert, 1929– Science project ideas.
QC161.2.G27 1997
533'.6' 078—dc21   97-7389
                                                              CIP
                                                              AC

Printed in the United States of America

10 9 8 7 6

Illustration Credits: Jacob Katari

Cover Photo: Jerry McCrea

CONTENTS

INTRODUCTION

In this book you will find experiments about air—the sea in which we live. The experiments use simple everyday materials you can find at home or at school.

The book will help you to work the way real scientists do. You will be answering questions by doing experiments to understand basic scientific principles.

Most of the experiments will provide detailed guidance. But some of them will raise questions and ask you to make up your own experiments to answer them. This is the kind of experiment that could be a particularly good start for a science fair project. Such experiments are marked with an asterisk (*).

Please note: **If an experiment uses anything that has a potential for danger, you will be asked to work with an adult.** *Please do so! The purpose of this teamwork is to prevent you from getting hurt.*

Science Project Ideas About Air *can open science's door for you—and make you glad that you live at the bottom of a sea of air!*

MEASUREMENT ABBREVIATIONS

atmosphere	atm	**inch**	in
centimeter	cm	**kilometer**	km
cubic millimeter	cu mm	**liter**	L
cubic kilometer	cu km	**meter**	m
degrees Celsius	°C	**mile**	mi
degrees Fahrenheit	°F	**milliliter**	ml
foot	ft	**millimeter**	mm
gallon	gal	**ounce**	oz
gram	g	**quart**	qt

No stir in the air, no stir in the sea,
The ship was still as she could be.

(Robert Southey)

1

THE SEA OF AIR IN WHICH WE LIVE

Suppose you were an alien traveling through space in a giant spaceship. You notice a star—the star we call our sun. You see that there are spheres (planets) that seem to be moving slowly about the star. You guide the ship near the sphere closest to the sun (Mercury). You find that it has a scorched surface where daytime temperatures reach 350°C (660°F). At night, the temperature falls to -170°C (-275°F) because there is very little gas and no water to hold the heat. Mercury has lost any atmosphere it may have had because its gravity is too weak to prevent fast-moving air molecules from escaping and spreading through space.

Moving farther from the sun, you meet the sphere that earthlings call Venus. Its surface is hot enough to melt silver—about 480°C (900°F). It is hot because its atmosphere is almost entirely carbon dioxide. The carbon dioxide creates what is called a greenhouse effect. The gas absorbs much of the planet's radiated heat and reflects it back to the surface. (Many scientists believe that increasing amounts of carbon dioxide in our own atmosphere are causing Earth's surface temperature to rise.) Later, as you approach the surface of this sphere, you find the pressure of its atmosphere is very large (90 times greater than Earth's). You decide it is not a good place to land, so you speed away to another sphere we call Mars. (You might wonder why your spaceship missed Earth on its way to Mars. The reason was that at that particular time Earth was on the other side of the sun.)

On Mars you find a barren desert surface with a thin atmosphere composed mostly of carbon dioxide. The pressure of this atmosphere is only 1/100 of the pressure you later find on Earth. The temperature ranges from a pleasant 20°C (68°F) to a very chilly -140°C (-220°F). Any water that existed on Mars is now frozen. Its white polar caps are probably a mixture of ice (frozen water) and dry ice (frozen carbon dioxide). What you thought were clouds as you approached the sphere known to earthlings as the Red Planet turned out to be giant dust storms. The dust storms indicate that there are winds on Mars. Since the air there is so thin, you realize that the particles of red dust moved by the winds are very tiny.

Upon leaving Mars, you see reflected light from the sphere we call Earth. It has emerged from behind the sun. It gleams in the sunlight like a bright blue marble. Its beauty attracts you and you decide to explore this bright blue sphere that you missed before. As you approach Earth, you see that it, like Venus, has clouds. But these clouds do not cover its entire surface. Between the clouds you can see patches of blue, green, yellow, and brown. You land on a patch of green and proceed to measure its atmosphere. This time you find a pressure similar to the one in your spaceship. You discover that this atmosphere has very little carbon dioxide, but it does have a vital gas that was lacking on the other spheres you explored. It has oxygen. In fact, one fifth of its atmosphere is oxygen! Your computer provides a table like Table 1. It shows the makeup of the three atmospheres you have sampled.

The other startling discovery is that Earth's atmosphere contains water, and much of its surface is covered with water. You realize that this sphere is much like the one from which you started your journey into space. You know that on your own planet, oxygen is produced by green plants—plants that have leaves and a green pigment that earthlings call chlorophyll. These plants are able to combine the small

 TABLE 1

GASES IN THREE PLANETS' ATMOSPHERES
(~ means approximately)

GAS	VENUS	EARTH	MARS
Nitrogen (N_2)	3%	78%	3%
Oxygen (O_2)	~0	21%	~0
Carbon dioxide (CO_2)	97%	0.03%	95%
Other gases	~0	~1%	~2%

amounts of carbon dioxide in the atmosphere with water to make food. At the same time, they release oxygen into the atmosphere. In fact, your spaceship carries green plants that you brought from home. It is these plants that have provided the oxygen you need to breathe.

The presence of oxygen in this sphere's atmosphere leads you to believe that living things may be here. Sure enough! You soon find an abundance of green plants. Later, you find animals that feed on these plants. You even find animals that resemble you; animals that have built their own spaceships. But these animals have not yet learned how to travel through the vast distances of their galaxy or universe. They have no time machine. Should you share your discovery with them?

Back to Reality

The events just described are fiction. So far as we know, aliens have not landed on Earth. However, the information about the atmospheres of Venus, Mars, and Earth is true. It is the oxygen in our atmosphere that makes it possible for us to live here. And it is green plants that produce this oxygen as they make their own food from carbon dioxide and water. Three billion years of living things on Earth have produced the oxygen we now breathe.

We call the mixture of gases that make up our atmosphere "air." Table 2 lists the gases found in air. Water vapor can make up as much as 5 percent of air, and the water content of air varies greatly from day to day and place to place. For that reason, Table 2 shows the composition of dry air. Dry air is air from which all the water has been removed. In addition to the gases listed in Table 2, air also contains traces of other gases; among them are ozone (O_3), carbon monoxide (CO), sulfur dioxide (SO_2), and radon (Rn).

Argon, neon, helium, krypton, xenon, and radon are gaseous elements called the noble or rare gases. They used to be called the inert gases because it was believed that they would not react with other elements. However, it has been found that some of these gases can be made to react with other elements under certain conditions.

Argon, which is used in lightbulbs, is the only noble gas to make up a significant part of the atmosphere. Helium is used in balloons and blimps. Neon and krypton are used to make colored light in electric signs. Radon is a harmful radioactive gas that sometimes collects in buildings. It can cause lung cancer.

TABLE 2

COMPOSITION OF DRY AIR

GAS	CHEMICAL FORMULA	PERCENT BY VOLUME*
nitrogen	N_2	78.09
oxygen	O_2	20.95
argon	Ar	0.93
carbon dioxide	CO_2	0.03
neon	Ne	0.0018
helium	He	0.00052
krypton	Kr	0.0001
hydrogen	H_2	0.00005
xenon	Xe	0.000008

Total exceeds 100 because numbers have been rounded.

Carbon dioxide, ozone, carbon monoxide, and sulfur dioxide make up only small fractions of our atmosphere, but they are the major contributors to air pollution. Sulfur dioxide is produced by burning coal and oil. It combines with water in the air to form an acid. If the acid condenses into raindrops, it makes up part of the acid rain that falls on parts of the country. Acid rain destroys trees, plants, and buildings. Sulfur dioxide can also be dangerous to people with breathing problems.

Carbon monoxide is produced by gasoline-burning engines in motor vehicles and by burning cigarettes. It combines with a chemical (hemoglobin) in our blood and reduces the amount of oxygen traveling from our lungs to the cells of our bodies. Its amount can increase to dangerous levels in heavy traffic and stagnant air. Breathing a heavy concentration of carbon monoxide can be fatal.

Close to Earth's surface, ozone makes up part of the smog that appears in large cities where there is bright sunlight and motor vehicle exhaust fumes. The ozone in smog can be very irritating to the eyes. Ozone is also found in the upper atmosphere. There it absorbs the sun's ultraviolet light. Without the upper atmosphere's ozone layer, much more ultraviolet light would reach Earth's surface. Ultraviolet light is capable of damaging living cells, and it is sometimes used to destroy harmful bacteria. However, it can also damage cells in our skin and cause skin cancer. Recently the amount of ozone in the upper atmosphere has been decreasing. Reduced amounts of ozone means that additional ultraviolet light can reach Earth and cause more skin cancer.

The decrease in ozone is believed to be caused by certain chemicals, such as Freon gas, which is used in spray cans, in air conditioners, and for other purposes. Freon slowly spreads into the upper atmosphere, where it slowly decomposes, releasing chlorine atoms. These atoms react with the ozone and change it to oxygen, which is not a good absorber of ultraviolet light. For this reason, Freon is no longer being made in the United States.

The Sea of Air

 You may not know it, but we live at the bottom of a vast sea. The sea we live in is much deeper than any ocean. We live in a sea of air called the "atmosphere."

It is in this air, within 12 km (7 mi) of Earth's surface, that we see clouds. Here raindrops and snowflakes grow and fall to the bottom of the sea of air. It is in this lower part of the atmosphere that winds blow, temperature and air pressure change, and tornadoes, hurricanes, and thunderstorms are produced.

On the bottom of the sea of air, at Earth's surface, our eyes sting from smog produced by automobiles and from industrial smoke. It is here that we have droughts, fog, mud, and deep snow. At the bottom of this sea we also enjoy the beauty of the air above and around us—clear blue skies, fluffy cottonlike clouds, soothing breezes, frost-covered grass and windowpanes, colorful sunsets, rainbows, and halos.

UP! UP! Into the Atmosphere

 Experiments using weather balloons, high-altitude airplanes, and rockets have shown that air pressure decreases as we go up into the atmosphere. You may have felt this decrease in pressure after taking off in an airplane or ascending to the top of a tall building in an elevator.

These experiments have shown, too, that temperature decreases with altitude. You may have noticed that it is usually cooler on a mountaintop than in the valley below. After a certain height in the atmosphere is reached, however, the temperature begins to increase again.

Meteorologists—scientists who study weather—have divided the atmosphere into layers (see Figure 1). The first layer, the one closest to the ground, is called the troposphere. Here the temperature drops as you go up. At the top of the troposphere, about 12 km (8 mi) from the ground, the temperature is -60°C (-76°F). The height of this lowest layer of the atmosphere changes with the time of year and the distance from the equator. Near the

FIGURE 1

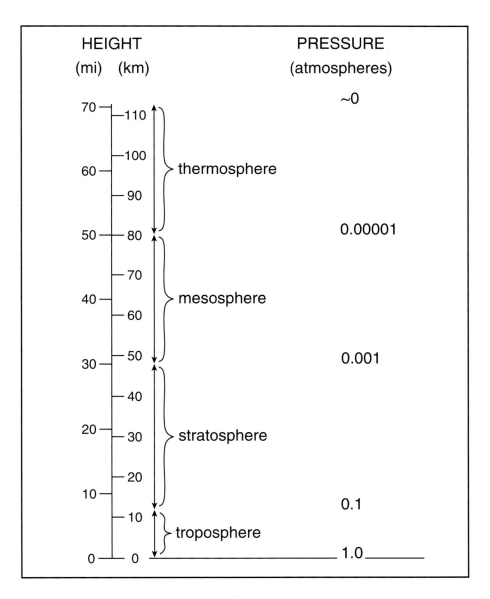

This chart shows the layers of Earth's atmosphere with their ranges of height and pressure.

equator, the troposphere is about 18 km (11 mi) tall. Near the North and South Poles, it is only about 6 km (4 mi) tall. The troposphere stretches higher in the summer.

Above the troposphere is the stratosphere, where the temperature rises with altitude to a maximum of about -5°C (23°F). Most of Earth's ozone is found in the stratosphere. Although there is very little of this gas in the atmosphere, it plays a very important role. It absorbs much of the ultraviolet light in sunlight. (It is the absorption of ultraviolet rays from the sun that warms the stratosphere.)

The stratosphere reaches to about 50 km (30 mi) from the ground, where we enter the mesosphere. Here the temperature falls again from -5°C (23°F) to -90°C (-130°F), and the altitude increases to 80 km (50 mi). Finally, in the thermosphere, at the top of Earth's atmosphere, the temperature rises again from -90°C to -35°C (-31°F) at an altitude of about 110 km (70 mi).

Although temperatures rise and fall as we ascend into the atmosphere, air pressure continues to fall the higher into the atmosphere we go. Air pressure just about halves for every 5.5 km (3.4 mi) of altitude. Rising through the troposphere, the pressure falls from 1.0 atmosphere (atm), the pressure at sea level, to 1/10 (0.1) atm. At the top of the stratosphere, air pressure is only 1/1,000 (0.001) atm. Through the mesosphere, the pressure falls to 1/100,000 (0.00001) atm. For all practical purposes, the air pressure is zero in the thermosphere.

The "thinner" air at high altitudes makes it harder to breathe. At the tops of peaks in the Rocky Mountains, the altitude is commonly 3,700 m (12,000 ft). On these mountains, even walking makes your heart beat fast and your breathing become rapid. The low air pressure on these mountains means that you take in less oxygen with each breath. You have to breathe faster to get the oxygen you need. Your heart must beat faster to carry the reduced oxygen in your blood to the rest of your body.

With time, you can adjust to high altitude. You become acclimatized. Your body produces more red blood cells. The added cells allow more oxygen to move from your lungs to the cells of your body. You also learn to take deeper breaths so that more oxygen enters your lungs. The people who live in the Andes Mountains of South America are able to work at an altitude of 5,800 m (19,000 ft) without ill effects. At this altitude, both the air pressure and the concentration of oxygen are less than half that at sea level. Blood tests show that these people have almost twice as many red blood cells as normal. Their lungs are also bigger and have more surface area. This makes it possible for more of the oxygen they breathe to get into their blood.

Jet airplanes, which fly at high altitudes, have pressurized air inside the plane to prevent passengers from feeling sick or short of breath. Another way to prevent high-altitude sickness is to provide oxygen-enriched air. In *Skylab,* an American space station used in 1973, the air the astronauts breathed had a pressure of only one third of an atmosphere. Normally, people cannot live in such air. It is the same as the air pressure at an altitude of 8,500 m (28,000 ft). But the astronauts were perfectly healthy there because the air they breathed was 70 percent oxygen at the reduced pressure. Ordinary air is only 21 percent oxygen. At the air pressure in *Skylab,* they were breathing the equivalent of air with 23 percent oxygen at normal atmospheric pressure.

Are melted into air, into thin air.
(William Shakespeare)

2

HOW DO WE KNOW THERE IS AIR?

We can't see air; we can't smell air; we can't taste air. So how do we know that air exists?

Even though we can't see, smell, or taste air, we can feel it. When the wind blows, you feel something moving over your skin. When you ride your bike or run, you feel something pushing against the skin on your face. Sometimes you can hear air as it rushes from a pump or hose. You can also hear the wind howl.

There are other ways of knowing that air exists. The experiments in this chapter will help you to believe that air is real.

DID YOU KNOW. . .?

When air is first compressed and then allowed to expand, it cools. By doing this over and over, air can be cooled to a temperature at which it condenses into a liquid at about -200°C (-328°F).

Experiment 2.1

AIR ON WATER

To do this experiment you will need:

- ✔ basin or sink
- ✔ wide-mouthed jar
- ✔ water
- ✔ small cork or piece of Styrofoam

Fill a basin or sink with water. Take an "empty" jar or bottle, turn it upside down, and push its open mouth down into the water, as shown in Figure 2a. Slowly push the jar deeper into the water. Does water move into the jar as you push it into the water? Does the water level outside the jar stay even with the water level inside the jar? What evidence do you have that there is something inside the jar?

Keeping the mouth of the jar underwater, slowly turn the jar on its side (see Figure 2b). Watch the mouth of the bottle closely. As water enters the jar, do you see anything coming out of the jar? Do you have evidence that a gas (perhaps air) was in the jar?

FIGURE 2

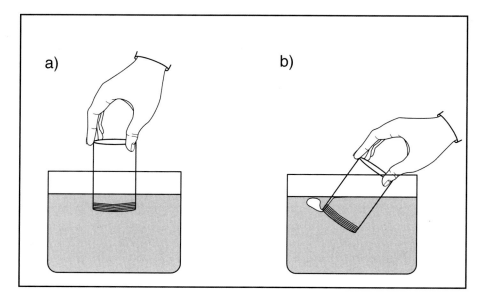

a) Push the mouth of an "empty" jar down into a container of water. Is anything in the jar?

b) Keeping the mouth of a jar underwater, slowly turn the jar on its side. What do you see coming out of the jar?

Put a small cork or a small piece of Styrofoam on the surface of a water-filled basin or sink. Turn an "empty" wide-mouthed jar upside down and lower it over the cork. Then push the jar down into the water. Do the cork and the water on which it is floating remain level with the water outside the jar? What evidence do you have that there really is something inside the "empty" jar?

Experiment 2.2

AIR PUSHING WATER OUT OF THE WAY

To do this experiment you will need:

- ✔ small plastic bag
- ✔ basin or sink
- ✔ water
- ✔ 2 wide-mouthed jars or bottles
- ✔ a partner

Hold open the mouth of a small plastic bag and drag it a short distance across a room. Twist shut the open end of the bag and hold it closed. Use your other hand to gently squeeze the part of the bag that has been sealed off. How do you know you have captured something in the bag? Perhaps that something is air.

Have a partner hold the sealed bag while you fill a basin or sink with water. Put a wide-mouthed jar or bottle under the water. Turn the jar so that it fills with water. Have your partner hold the water-filled jar upside down with its mouth underwater, as shown in Figure 3. Hold the closed plastic bag so that its mouth is inside the mouth of the jar. Untwist the bag and gently squeeze the gas in the bag.

FIGURE 3

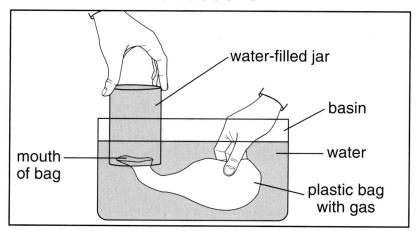

water-filled jar

basin

mouth of bag

water

plastic bag with gas

A gas from a plastic bag displaces water in a jar.

What comes out of the bag? What happens to the water inside the jar?

Find a second wide-mouthed jar similar to the one you just used. Place one jar in the basin or sink and fill it with water. Turn and hold it so that it is upside down and remains full with its mouth underwater (see Figure 4a). Turn the second empty jar upside down. Push its open mouth down into the water. As you found before, air in the jar prevents water from entering. Now carefully tip the second jar so that air coming out of its mouth can enter the water-filled jar above it (see Figure 4b). Notice how the air from the second jar displaces the water in the first one you are holding upside down.

Figure 4

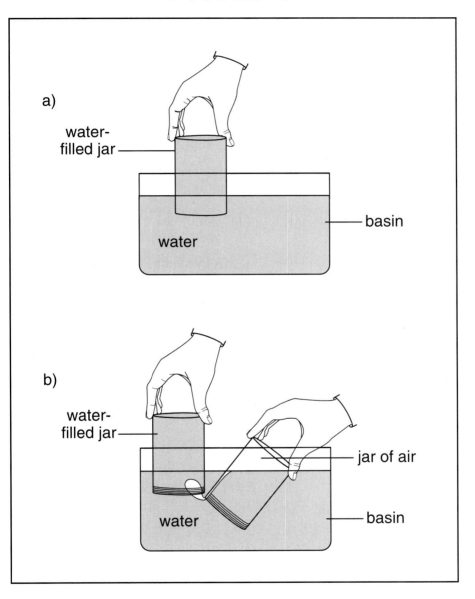

a) A water-filled jar is shown with its mouth underwater.

b) Air from one jar displaces water in another.

Experiment *2.3

CAN YOU WEIGH AIR?

To do this experiment you will need:

- ✔ an ADULT
- ✔ laboratory balance from your school or a balance you can build from a yardstick, drill and bit (1/8 in), nail, paper clips, string, and clay
- ✔ basin or sink
- ✔ plastic bags
- ✔ twisties
- ✔ air pump
- ✔ water
- ✔ container to hold water
- ✔ balloons (9-in or larger)
- ✔ measuring cup
- ✔ spring balance (0–100g)
- ✔ aluminum pie plates
- ✔ soccer ball, volleyball, football, or playground ball
- ✔ weights (containers of water, or stones)

To find out if air has weight, you will need a balance. You may be able to use one at your school. If not, you can make a simple but sensitive balance of your own.

To build a balance, **ASK AN ADULT** to drill three small holes through a yardstick at the points shown in Figure 5a. Be sure the hole at the 18-in mark is above the center of the balance beam (yardstick). The two holes at each end of the balance (at the 1-in and 35-in

FIGURE 5

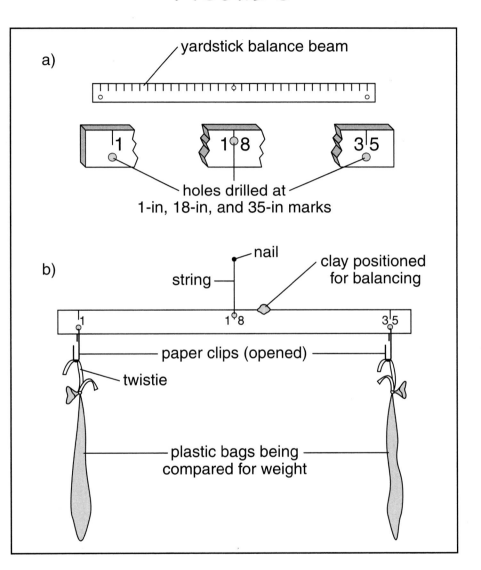

a) You can make a balance beam from a yardstick.

b) Use a string to suspend the beam from a nail. Add an unfolded paper clip at each end of the beam so that you can compare the weights of different objects by hanging them from opposite ends of the beam. If necessary, add a small lump of clay to one side of the beam to make it level.

marks) should be near the bottom of the beam, as shown.

Insert a string through the middle hole. Use the string to hang the balance beam from a long, strong nail (see Figure 5b). Open two paper clips. Put the wider end of each opened paper clip through the holes at each end of the balance. If the balance beam (yardstick) is not quite level, add a small piece of clay to the lighter (higher) side. Move the clay closer to or farther from the center of the beam until the yardstick is level. To compare the weights of two objects, hang them from the lower ends of the two paper clips.

If you are using a laboratory balance, weigh an empty plastic bag and a twistie. Then pull the bag through the air to fill it. Seal it with the twistie and reweigh it.

If you are using a yardstick balance, squeeze any enclosed air from two identical plastic bags. Use twisties to hang the two bags from opposite ends of the balance beam. Next, open the mouth of one bag and pull it through air to fill it. Use the same twistie to seal the bag and hang it from the same end of the balance as before. Does the bag weigh more when filled with air?

To see why the weight of the bag didn't change when you filled it with air, think of what would happen if you tried to weigh water in water. Better yet, you can weigh a balloon filled with water in air and then in water.

Take a large balloon (9-in or larger) and fill it with water using a measuring cup, as shown in Figure 6a. Be sure the balloon is completely filled and without air bubbles. Then seal the neck of the balloon with a twistie (see Figure 6b). Use one end of the twistie to hang the water-filled balloon from a spring balance (see Figure 6c). (Your school probably has a spring balance that you can use.) How much does the water-filled balloon weigh in air?

Next, weigh the water-filled balloon when it is in water, as shown in Figure 6d. How much does it weigh in water?

You were probably not surprised to find that water weighs nothing (or nearly nothing) when weighed in water. After all, if you float in water, you weigh nothing in water. The water pushes upward on the water-filled balloon just as it does on you when you float in water.

The same thing holds true in air. A bag of air weighs nothing because it is supported by the air it pushes out of the way. This support is called buoyancy. It is similar to the upward push on a balloonful of water that is submerged in water. The upward push on the water balloon equals the weight of the water in the

FIGURE 6

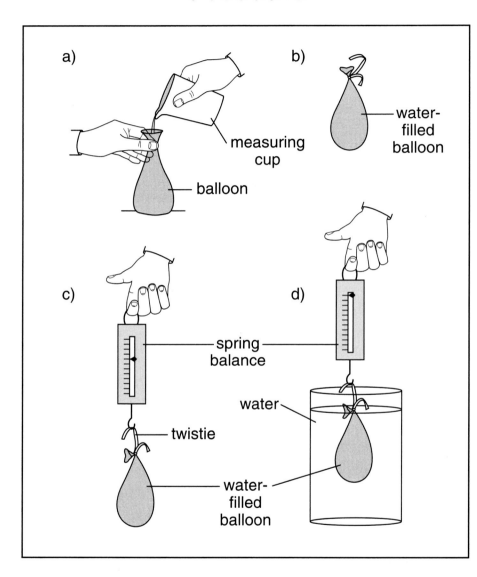

a) Use a measuring cup to fill a balloon with water.

b) Seal the balloon with a twistie.

c) Weigh the water-filled balloon in air.

d) Weigh the water-filled balloon in water.

balloon. Since the weight pulling the water balloon down equals the buoyant force pushing the same balloon up, the balloon has no weight in water. Similarly, a bag of air weighs nothing in air.

Suppose we force air into a balloon instead of filling an unstretchable plastic bag with air. Will an air-filled balloon weigh anything?

Blow up a large balloon (9-in or larger). Hold the balloon closed, but release air slowly through its neck. Air rushes from the balloon. It comes out of the balloon because it has a pressure greater than the air outside the balloon. That is, the outward push of the air inside the balloon is greater than the inward push of the air outside the balloon. You can feel and hear the air flowing from the balloon.

If you are using a laboratory balance, weigh an empty balloon. Then fill the balloon with air, tie a knot in the balloon's neck, and reweigh it. If you are using a yardstick balance, use identical twisties to hang two identical balloons (9-in or larger) from opposite ends of the balance. If the beam is not quite level, move a small piece of clay along the yardstick until the beam is level. Then blow up one of the balloons. Seal its neck with the twistie and hang it from the balance beam as before. Does the air-filled balloon weigh more than the empty balloon? How can you tell?

Suppose you filled the balloon by blowing air into it. Any increase in weight might be due to the fact that air coming from your lungs is not the same as the air you breathe. Perhaps "lung air" is heavier than regular air. Or perhaps the weight is caused by saliva you left on the balloon. What can you do so that you know the balloon is filled with air and not "lung air" and saliva?

Find a soccer ball, a volleyball, a football, or a playground ball. Let the air out of the ball (deflate it) and weigh it. If you are using a yardstick balance, you will need to make pans for your balance. Figure 7 shows you how to do this. Place the deflated ball on one pan of a balance. Place weights, containers of water, or stones on the other pan until the beam (yardstick) is level.

Next, use an air pump to fill the ball with air. Pump air into the ball until it is hard. If you have a pressure gauge, pump air into the ball until the pressure agrees with the pressure printed on the ball. Place the inflated ball back on the balance. Does air have weight? How can you tell?

FIGURE 7

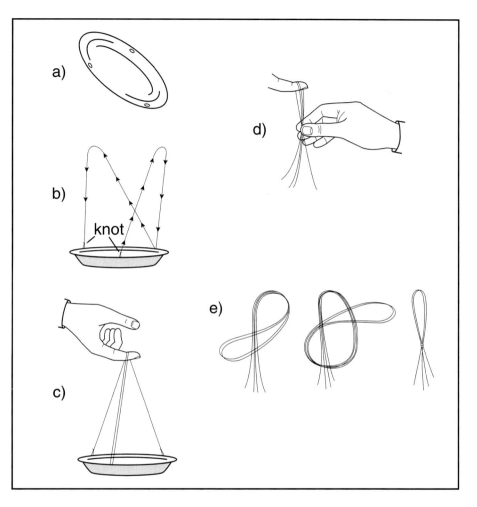

a) To make a pan for a yardstick balance, **ASK AN ADULT** to punch three equally-spaced holes near the edge of an aluminum pie plate.

b) Loop a 1.2-m length of string through the holes and tie the ends as shown.

c) Insert a finger through the two loops of string and slide the string until the pan hangs level.

d) Pinch off a loop of string near the top of the loops.

e) Tie this loop into a knot so it can be hung from the paper clip at the end of the balance beam.

Air Is Real

 From the experiments you have done, you have good evidence that air exists. You have seen that there is something in a jar that appears to be empty. You know something is there, because when you push its open mouth down into water, water does not enter the jar. Air fills the space in the jar and water cannot get in.

If you pull an open plastic bag through the space around you, you can close off the bag and feel that there is something in the bag. The gas in the bag resists being squeezed; it takes up space inside the bag. If you open the same bag, you can squeeze the gas into a water-filled jar. The gas will displace (push out) the water from the jar.

You have also seen that you can weigh air. When you squeezed air (put it under pressure) into a balloon or an inflatable ball, you found that the weight of the balloon or ball increased. This showed you that air has weight. But it didn't tell you how much a liter of ordinary air weighs.

Chemists weigh air by using a pump to remove air from a strong glass jar. This creates a vacuum inside the jar. A valve is used to close off the jar so that no air can enter. The truly empty jar is weighed, and the weight is recorded. The valve is then opened so that air can enter the jar. When the jar is reweighed, it is found to weigh more. If the jar has a volume of 1.0 L, its weight will increase by about 1.2 g. The weight of 1.0 L of air will be affected by its pressure and temperature. A liter of warm air weighs less than a liter of cold air. Air weighed on a mountaintop, where the pressure is less, will not weigh as much as air weighed at sea level.

The results of some experiments in which different gases were weighed in a room where the pressure was 1.0 atmosphere (76 cm, or 30 in of mercury, or 1.013 bar) and the temperature was 20°C (68°F) are shown in Table 3. The weights are given in grams (g). The weights of

TABLE 3

WEIGHTS OF 1.0 L OF SEVERAL DIFFERENT GASES

GAS	WEIGHT OF 1.0 L
air	1.20 g
argon	1.66 g
carbon dioxide	1.83 g
helium	0.17 g
hydrogen	0.08 g
nitrogen	1.17 g
oxygen	1.33 g
sulfur dioxide	2.67 g

the gases were found by first weighing a 1.0-L flask from which all the air had been removed. A gas was then allowed to enter the flask. The flask was sealed and reweighed. The weight of the gas was found by subtracting the weight of the empty flask from the weight of the gas-filled flask.

Which of the gases in Table 3 is the heaviest per liter (densest)? Which gas in the table weighs the least per liter (least dense)? Which gases are heavier (more dense) than air? Which gases are lighter (less dense) than air?

Experiment *2.4

CARBON DIOXIDE AND AIR

To do this experiment you will need:

- ✔ laboratory balance from your school or yardstick balance you built for Experiment 2.3
- ✔ seltzer tablets
- ✔ water
- ✔ measuring cup or medicine cup
- ✔ small, clear flask or bottle (an empty aspirin bottle that holds 250 tablets works well)
- ✔ 3 balloons (9-in or larger) of different colors
- ✔ paper towels
- ✔ twisties
- ✔ bicycle tire pump

Table 3 indicates that an equal volume of carbon dioxide is heavier than air. To see if it really is heavier, you can compare the weights of equal volumes of air and carbon dioxide.

You can make some carbon dioxide by dropping seltzer tablets into water. The seltzer reacts with the water to form bubbles of carbon dioxide gas that you can collect.

Put about 30 ml (1 oz) of water in a small, clear flask or bottle (an empty aspirin bottle that holds 250 tablets works fine). Break two seltzer tablets in half. Drop them into the water and pull the neck of a balloon over the top of the flask. The carbon dioxide gas will blow up the balloon as the gas is produced in the flask.

Gently swirl the flask to free as many carbon dioxide bubbles as possible. When the reaction is over, seal the neck of the balloon with a twistie and remove the balloon from the flask. Dry the mouth of the balloon with a paper towel.

Use a bicycle tire pump to fill a second balloon of the same size but a different color with air. Inflate it to the same size as the one with carbon dioxide. Seal the neck of the air-filled balloon with a twistie. Hang both balloons from opposite ends of the yardstick balance, or weigh them separately on a laboratory balance. Is carbon dioxide heavier (more dense) than air?

You may have heard that the gas you exhale (breathe out) from your lungs contains carbon dioxide. Do you think lung air is as heavy (dense) as carbon dioxide? Do you think it is heavier (more dense) than air?

You can find out by blowing your lung air into a third balloon of a different color than the first two. Inflate it to the same size as the air- and carbon dioxide-filled balloons. Then seal its neck with a twistie. Use a paper towel to wipe off any saliva that might be in the neck of the balloon.

Compare the weights of the three balloons on your yardstick balance or on a laboratory balance. Is lung air as heavy (dense) as an equal volume of carbon dioxide? Is it heavier (denser) than an equal volume of air?

DID YOU KNOW. . .?

People sometimes refer to damp air as "heavy air." Actually, damp (wet) air is less dense than dry air. The reason is that the density (weight per volume) of water vapor is less than the density of air. This fact is reflected by the low pressure that usually accompanies stormy weather.

3
AIR,
TEMPERATURE,
AND PRESSURE

Temperature is a measure of how warm or cold something is. It is measured with a thermometer. The most common use of a thermometer is to measure air temperature. When the air is cold, heat flows from your body to the cold air. You try to reduce heat loss from your body by wearing layers of clothing. When the air is hot, heat flows more slowly from your body. You may even produce heat inside your body faster than it flows out. If the air is warmer than your body, heat will flow from the air into your body. In either case, you will sweat. The evaporation of sweat helps to cool your body.

Pressure is the push (force) that something exerts on the area that it touches. When you stand on a floor, the pressure you exert on the floor is your weight spread over the area of the soles of your feet. Pressure can be measured in newtons per square meter, pounds per square inch, or other units. A barometer can be used to measure air pressure.

Experiment *3.1

AIR AND TEMPERATURE

To do this experiment you will need:

- ✔ thermometer
- ✔ building with basement and attic and an outside area
- ✔ blacktop area with grassy area nearby

You can measure temperature with a thermometer. On a bright sunny day, take a thermometer outside and measure the temperature of the air in different places. Be sure you leave the thermometer in each place for several minutes. The liquid level in the thermometer should not be changing when you read the thermometer.

Go outside and measure the temperature on the north side of a building such as your house or school. Then measure the temperature on the south side of the same building. How do the temperatures compare? Can you explain any differences?

How does the air temperature over blacktop compare with the air temperature over a grassy area nearby? How does the temperature in a sunny area compare with the temperature in a shady place?

During the same day, measure the temperature on the east and west side of the building. Do this at different times of the same day. How do these temperatures compare? Can you explain any differences?

If it is spring or fall when the building is not being heated or cooled, measure some temperatures inside. How do the air temperatures in the basement, on the ground floor, and in the attic compare? Can you explain any differences in temperature that you find at these various levels?

Measure the temperature near the floor of a room. Then measure the temperature near the ceiling. How do these two temperatures compare? Can you explain any difference in temperature that you find at these different levels in the room?

Experiment 3.2

AIR AND PRESSURE: A BOUNCING COIN

To do this experiment you will need:

✔ basin or pail

✔ sink

✔ narrow-necked glass bottle

✔ water

✔ coin

✔ hot and cold tap water

Place a small plastic pail or basin in a large sink. Stand an empty narrow-necked glass bottle upright in the pail or basin. Moisten the mouth of the bottle with a wet finger. Then completely cover the mouth of the bottle with a coin, as shown in Figure 8. Place your hands around the bottle to warm it. Watch and listen closely. You may see and hear the coin lift and fall back onto the mouth of the bottle.

If you can't produce enough heat with your hands, let hot tap water run into the basin or pail and again watch the coin closely. You will see and hear the coin lift and fall back onto the bottle's mouth. Can you explain why the coin does this? Does this experiment provide any evidence that there is a gas in the bottle? What

FIGURE 8

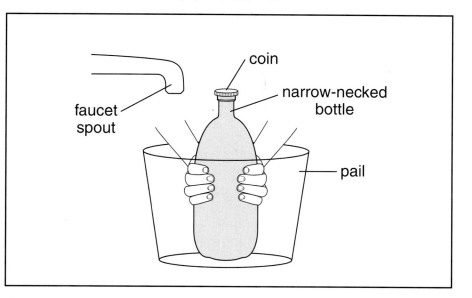

First try to use just your hands to increase air pressure and make a coin bounce.

do you think will happen if you repeat the experiment and let cold tap water run into the basin or pail?

As you saw, when air is heated, its pressure increases. The pressure of the warm gas became large enough to lift the coin covering the mouth of the bottle. The force of the air pushing upward on the coin became greater than the weight of the coin and the force of the air pushing it downward. What else happens to a gas when it is heated? The next experiment will help you answer that question.

Experiment *3.3

AIR, TEMPERATURE, AND EXPANSION

To do this experiment you will need:

- ✔ small plastic bag
- ✔ large (1-L) wide-mouthed glass jar
- ✔ rubber band
- ✔ freezer
- ✔ pail or basin
- ✔ sink
- ✔ hot tap water

Place the open end of a small plastic bag around a large wide-mouthed glass jar. Use a rubber band to hold the bag firmly against the mouth of the jar. Be sure no air can get into or out of the jar and bag. Place the jar and attached plastic bag in a freezer, where the air in the bottle will become very cold.

After about ten minutes, place a pail or basin in a sink. Partially fill the pail or basin with hot tap water. Then remove the jar and bag from the freezer. Hold the jar upright with the lower half of it submerged in the hot tap water. What happens to the plastic bag as the air in the jar warms? What happens to air when its temperature rises?

To see what happens to air when its temperature decreases, put the jar and bag back into the freezer. After ten minutes, look at the jar and bag again. What has happened to the bag? What happens to air when its temperature falls?

DID YOU KNOW. . .?

When liquid air is allowed to warm, nitrogen boils (changes from liquid to gas) at -196°C (-321°F). Oxygen then boils at -183°C (-297°F).

Experiment *3.4

AIR, TEMPERATURE, AND PRESSURE

To do this experiment you will need:

- ✔ pail
- ✔ hot and cold tap water
- ✔ balloons
- ✔ 2-L bottle
- ✔ pencil with eraser
- ✔ freezer

You can do an experiment similar to the previous one using a balloon instead of a plastic bag. However, a balloon tends to squeeze air together. It increases the pressure of the air inside the balloon. If you let the balloon go, it whizzes around as air is squeezed from it. This happens because the pressure of the air inside the balloon is greater than the pressure of the air outside the balloon. The increased pressure is caused by the balloon's stretched rubber wall.

Pull the open end of an empty balloon over the mouth of a 2-L bottle, as shown in Figure 9. Put the bottle in a pail of hot tap water. What happens to the balloon? What happens to the volume of the air when its temperature rises?

How do you know that the pressure of the air increases as it gets warmer?

Remove the bottle from the hot water and let it cool for a few minutes. What happens to the balloon as the air in the bottle cools? How can you explain what happens?

Remove the balloon from the bottle. Rinse the bottle several times with hot water. The warm bottle will heat air entering the bottle after the water is poured out. Put the balloon back on the bottle of warm air. What happens to the balloon as the air inside the bottle cools?

FIGURE 9

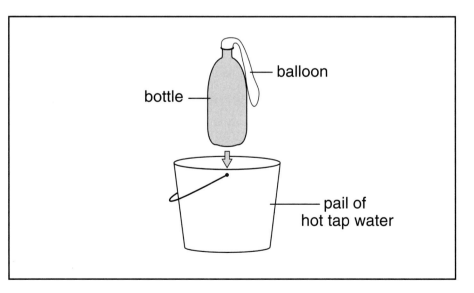

Use a bottle, balloon, and pail of water to find the effect of temperature on air volume and pressure.

The temperature of the air can be lowered some more by putting the bottle in a pail of cold water. What happens to the balloon as the air in the bottle continues to cool?

To cool the air even more, put the bottle in a freezer, where the temperature is well below 0°C (32°F). After about ten minutes, remove the bottle. What has happened to the balloon? What happened to the volume of the air in the bottle when its temperature dropped? What happened to its pressure?

Remove the bottle from the freezer. Predict what will happen as the temperature of the air in the bottle rises to room temperature. Were you right?

Or on wide-waving wings expanded bear
The flying-chariot through the fields of air.
(Erasmus Darwin)

4

AIR
PRESSURE

Since we live at the bottom of a sea of air, as we saw in Chapter 1, we should expect to experience the weight of that sea. We should find a pressure acting on us, a pressure caused by the tall column of air above us. We certainly feel an increasing pressure when we dive into water. The next experiment will show you the pressure in water, which will lead to evidence of air pressure.

Experiment *4.1

WATER PRESSURE

To do this experiment you will need:

- ✔ 2 large cans, such as coffee cans
- ✔ an ADULT
- ✔ hammer
- ✔ nail
- ✔ masking tape
- ✔ water
- ✔ sink

To see that water exerts a pressure, find two large cans. **ASK AN ADULT** to help you punch holes in the sides of the cans using a hammer and nail. Be sure the holes are the same size. In one can, punch one hole near the bottom, another near the top, and two in between, as shown in Figure 10a. In the second can, punch five or six holes approximately equal distances apart near the bottom of the can, as shown in Figure 10b. Use masking tape on the outside of the can to cover the holes in both cans.

Fill the two cans with water. Place the can with the holes arranged from top to bottom at the edge of a sink. Turn the can so that water

FIGURE 10

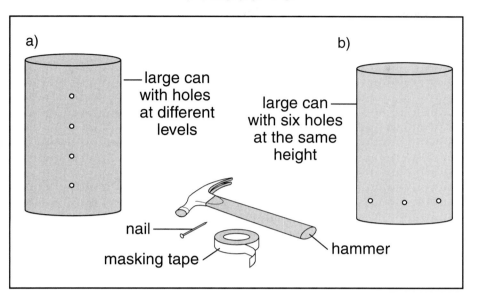

a) Holes punched in large cans may be used to show the difference in pressure at different depths of water.

b) They can also be used to show that at the same depth, pressure is equal in all directions.

coming out the holes will flow into the sink. Quickly remove the tape from the holes. From which hole does the water project farthest? What does this experiment tell you about pressure as you go deeper in water?

Next, take the can that has six holes punched around it near its bottom. Hold this can over the sink. Quickly remove the tape. How does the projection of water from each hole compare? What can you say about the pressure at the same depth in water? Does it seem to be equal in all directions?

Air Pressure and Barometers

 As you saw in the last experiment, pressure increases as you go deeper in water. But at any one depth, the pressure is equal in all directions. If you have an aneroid barometer, like the one shown in Figure 11a, you can explore the pressure at different depths in the sea of air. An aneroid barometer is not like a mercury barometer. A mercury barometer (see Figure 11b) contains liquid mercury. When the barometer is made, the long tube is filled with mercury. The open end is covered and the tube is turned upside down. The lower end of the tube is placed in a shallow well of mercury. When the cover is removed from the open end, the mercury level falls. Since nothing entered the tube as the mercury fell, the space in the tube above the mercury is truly empty. Except for a small amount of mercury vapor, it is a vacuum. If the barometer is at sea level on a normal day, the height of the mercury in the tube will be about 76 cm (30 in) above the mercury level in the well. This column of mercury pushing downward balances the pressure of the air pushing it upward. When air pressure

FIGURE 11

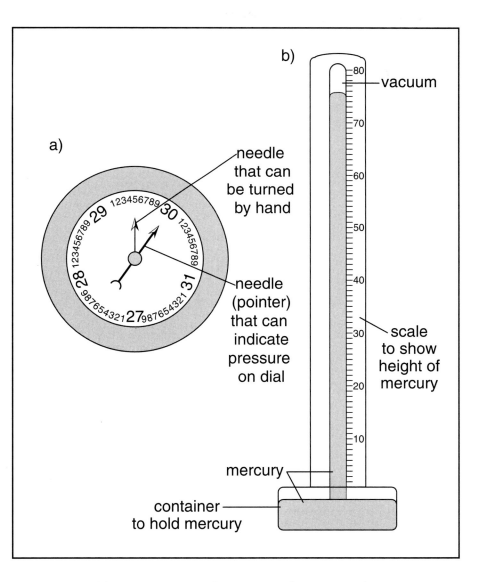

An aneroid barometer (a) and a mercury barometer (b) measure air pressure.

decreases, as it often does when a storm approaches, the height of the mercury column decreases, too.

Barometers can be made using water instead of mercury. But water barometers are not very convenient to read. Because mercury weighs more than 13.5 times as much as an equal volume of water, air pressure will support a column of water more than 10 m (34 ft) tall at sea level.

An aneroid barometer (see Figure 12) has a hole in the back where air can enter. The air pushes against a sealed, thin, round, hollow

FIGURE 12

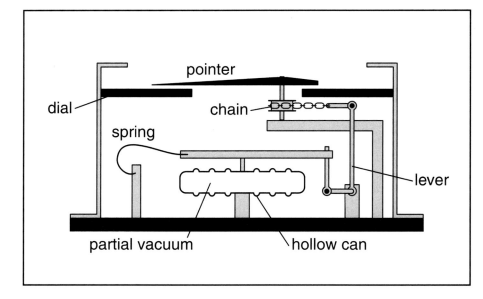

This diagram shows the inside of an aneroid barometer.

metal can. Most of the air has been pumped out of the can. The outside of the can is attached to a spring. A series of levers connects the spring to a chain that turns a pointer over the dial of the barometer.

When the air pressure increases, the sides of the can are pushed inward. The can then stretches the spring, which pulls on the chain and turns the pointer so that it points toward a larger number on the dial. When air pressure decreases, the sides of the can move outward, the spring is stretched less, and the pointer indicates a smaller number on the dial. Why do you think the dials on aneroid barometers seldom go below 26 (inches of mercury) or above 32?

Experiment *4.2

A BAROMETER IN WATER AND AIR

To do this experiment you will need:

- ✔ aneroid barometer
- ✔ sealable plastic bag
- ✔ pail
- ✔ water
- ✔ high hill or mountain
- ✔ car
- ✔ building with several flights of stairs and an elevator

Another way to show that pressure increases as you go down into water is to use an aneroid barometer. Place the barometer in a new sealable plastic bag. Seal the bag. Then watch the dial as you lower the barometer into a pail of water. What happens to the barometer reading as you lower it deeper into the pail?

Now that you've tested the barometer at different depths in water, you can carry it into the sea of air. If we live at the bottom of a sea of air, then we should expect to see the pressure of the air decrease as we go higher into the sea (atmosphere). You can do an experiment to see if this is true. Carry the barometer up a high hill or mountain. Read the barometer dial at the bottom and at the top of the hill or mountain. Does air pressure decrease as you go higher?

Take the barometer with you when you travel by car. Does air pressure increase as you go down a long hill? Does the air pressure decrease as you go up a hill?

What happens to the air pressure as you go up in an elevator? What happens to the pressure when you go down in an elevator? Can you detect any change in pressure when you climb a flight of stairs? Can you detect any change when you climb several flights of stairs?

Your experiments indicate that air pressure, like water pressure, increases as you go deeper into the sea of air. Design an experiment to show that at any point air pressure, like water pressure, is equal in all directions.

SOME AIR PRESSURE EFFECTS

To do this experiment you will need:

- ✔ 2 clear plastic drinking straws
- ✔ glass tumbler
- ✔ water
- ✔ finishing nail and a larger nail
- ✔ glass or rigid plastic bottle
- ✔ scissors
- ✔ paper towel
- ✔ sink
- ✔ empty coffee can with plastic cover

- ✔ empty soup can
- ✔ hammer
- ✔ masking tape
- ✔ petroleum jelly
- ✔ plastic kitchen funnel
- ✔ bottle with narrow neck
- ✔ cup
- ✔ clay
- ✔ paper clip
- ✔ plastic soda bottle with a narrow neck
- ✔ balloon (9-in or larger)

Air pressure explains a number of effects that may, at first, seem to be magic. You will investigate a few of these effects in this series of experiments.

A Drinking-Straw Pipette

Chemists use pipettes like the one shown in Figure 13a to transfer liquids from one container to another. You can make a pipette from a drinking straw. Lower a clear plastic drinking straw into a glass of water. Place your index finger or thumb firmly on the top of the straw, as shown in Figure 13b. Now lift the straw out of the water. Notice that the water stays in the straw. What happens when you remove your finger from the top of the straw?

FIGURE 13

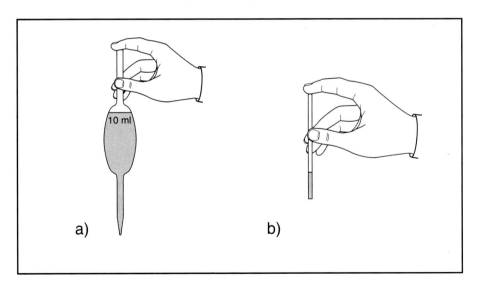

a)   b)

A chemist's pipette (a) or a simple drinking-straw pipette (b) can be used to transfer liquids.

A Holey Drinking Straw

Use another clear plastic straw to drink water from a glass. Then use a finishing nail to make a hole through the straw about 5 cm (2 in) below its upper end. What happens when you try to drink through the straw now? Can you drink through the straw if you cover the holes with your fingers? What do you think will happen if you try to use this holey straw as a pipette? Try it! Were you right?

The Amazing Upside-Down Bottle of Water

Fill a glass or rigid plastic bottle as full as possible with water. Use scissors to cut a piece of paper towel that is slightly larger than the mouth of the bottle. Place the paper on the mouth of the bottle. Turn the bottle upside down over a sink. You will find that the water stays in the bottle, as shown in Figure 14.

Two Ways to Prevent a Can from Leaking

Find an empty coffee can with a plastic cover that fits it snugly. Also find an empty soup can. **ASK AN ADULT** to use a hammer and nail to punch a hole in the

FIGURE 14

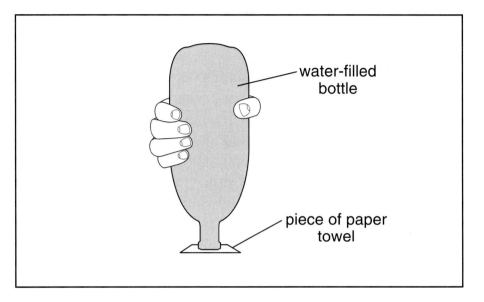

water-filled
bottle

piece of paper
towel

An ordinary piece of paper towel can keep water in an upside-down bottle.

side of each can near the bottom (see Figure 15). Cover the holes with masking tape. Fill the coffee can with water and place it on the edge of a sink. Use your finger to apply a thin layer of petroleum jelly around the inside of the lip on the plastic cover. The petroleum jelly will act as a seal so that air will not be able to enter the can when you put the cover on the can.

Remove the tape so that water begins to flow from the can and into the sink. Then put

FIGURE 15

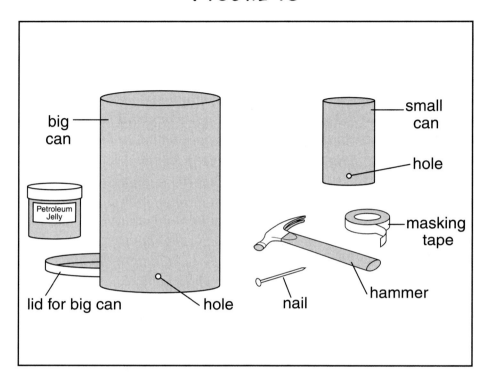

You can make a leakproof can.

the cover on the can. Twist the cover back and forth to make sure the petroleum jelly seals the can and air cannot enter. The water will stop flowing soon after you put the top on the can.

Repeat the experiment with the small can filled with water, but this time use your hand rather than a plastic lid to cover the can. Can you stop the flow of water with your hand?

A Funnel That Doesn't Work

Place the neck of a plastic kitchen funnel into the mouth of a bottle. Put some water in a cup. Pour the water into the funnel. You will find that the water runs freely through the funnel and into the bottle. Remove the funnel and place a ring of soft clay on the mouth of the bottle. Put the funnel back on the bottle. Be sure the clay seals the funnel so that air cannot pass between the bottle's mouth and the funnel (see Figure 16). What happens when you pour water into the funnel now?

FIGURE 16

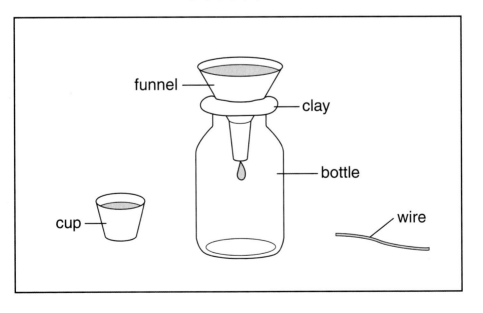

This funnel doesn't work.

Find a paper clip and open it so that it becomes a short length of wire. Gently push the wire through the clay to make a hole into the bottle. Air can now pass from the bottle. What happens to the water in the funnel?

A Balloon in a Bottle

Find a plastic soda bottle that has a narrow neck. Put the round part of a balloon in the bottle. Leave the mouth of the balloon outside the bottle. Try to blow up the balloon. You will find you can't blow the balloon up very much. Put a drinking straw into the bottle beside the balloon. Be sure the top of the straw is above the mouth of the bottle. You will find that it is much easier to blow up the balloon now until it fills the bottle.

Air Pressure Effects Explained

Air pressure can support a column of mercury 76 cm (30 in) high and a column of water 10 m (34 ft) tall, so it is not surprising that it can support a column of water in a bottle as it did in "The Amazing Upside-Down Bottle of Water." When the water in the drinking-straw pipette (in "A Drinking-Straw Pipette") starts to fall out of the straw, it slightly lengthens the air column below your finger. Because the volume of air above the water in the straw has grown slightly larger without any new air entering the straw, that air now exerts less pressure than the air below the water in the straw. Because the air pressure above the column of water in the straw is less than the air pressure around it, the water stays in the straw pipette. As soon as you remove your finger, air enters the top of the straw. This makes the air pressure above the water the same as the air pressure beneath it. The water's weight then causes it to fall. The same explanation applies to "Two Ways to Prevent a Can from Leaking." As water leaks from the covered can, the volume of air trapped above the water increases. This expansion reduces the air pressure in the can. When the sum of the pressures exerted by the air above the liquid and the liquid itself equals the air pressure outside the can, the water stops flowing.

For the opposite reason, you can't drink water through a straw that has a hole above the water level ("A Holey Drinking Straw"). When you drink liquid through a straw, you draw air out of the straw, creating a partial vacuum. The outside air pressure then becomes greater than the pressure in the straw, so water is pushed up the straw. If you make a hole near the top of the straw, air can enter the straw. Since the air pressure in the straw is the same as the air pressure on its outside, there is no force to push water up the straw.

The funnel doesn't work (in "A Funnel That Doesn't Work") because the water in the sealed funnel's spout compresses the volume of air in the bottle. The pressure of the trapped air rises, and it quickly equals the sum of the pressures of the small column of water and the air outside the bottle. For a similar reason, you can't blow up a balloon in a bottle ("A Balloon in a Bottle"). The air in the bottle is compressed by the balloon and quickly becomes equal to the pressure of your lungs. By placing a straw in the bottle, air trapped between the balloon and bottle can escape. Now the only pressure you have to overcome is air pressure and the resistance of the balloon.

AIR PRESSURE AND A CAN: ANOTHER EFFECT OF AIR PRESSURE

To do this experiment you will need:

- ✔ an ADULT
- ✔ water
- ✔ graduated cylinder or measuring cup
- ✔ stove
- ✔ clean, empty, aluminum soda can

- ✔ pair of heavy gloves, pot holders, or tongs
- ✔ medicine cup or measuring cup
- ✔ small plastic pail

If you had a vacuum pump, you could pump the air out of a metal can or drum and see what happens. You probably don't have a vacuum pump, but you can still see the effect of air pressure on a sealed metal can.

To begin, find a clean, empty, aluminum soda can. Ask an adult to help you with this experiment. Provide the adult with a pair of heavy gloves, pot holders, or tongs. Pour about 30 ml (1 oz) of water into the soda can. **ASK THE ADULT** to place the can with the small amount of water on a stove burner. While the can is heating, fill a small plastic pail with cold water and place it beside the stove. Let the water in the can boil for about a minute. You will see steam coming out of the can. **ASK THE ADULT** (wearing gloves or using tongs) to pick up the can, turn it upside down over the pail, and quickly lower it into the cold water.

You will hear the can pop as it is crushed by air pressure! The steam from the boiling water replaced the air in the can. When the can was suddenly cooled, the steam condensed quickly, reducing the pressure inside the can. The air pressure pushing inward on the can caused it to collapse.

Experiment 4.5

THE MAGDEBURG HEMISPHERES EXPERIMENT — A SMALLER VERSION

To do this experiment you will need:

- ✔ 5-cm (2-in) suction cups (from a hardware store)
- ✔ water
- ✔ pliers

In 1654, Otto von Guericke performed a demonstration for Emperor Ferdinand III in Regensburg, Germany. The experiment has become known as the experiment of the Magdeburg hemispheres (half a sphere or ball) because von Guericke built the hemispheres in his home town of Magdeburg. Von Guericke had invented an air pump that would pump air as well as water. In his famous experiment, he used two copper hemispheres, each 56 cm (22 in) in diameter. The hemispheres were placed together, with an airtight ring of leather soaked in oil and wax between them, to form a sphere.

Von Guericke used his air pump to remove the air from the inside of the sphere. He then hitched the opposite ends of the sphere to two eight-horse teams. Strain as they might, the horses could not pull the hemispheres apart (see Figure 17). The emperor and all who watched the experiment were amazed. Today we are less amazed because we can calculate the force of the air pressure holding them together. It was nearly three tons!

You can do a miniature Magdeburg hemisphere experiment using suction cups

FIGURE 17

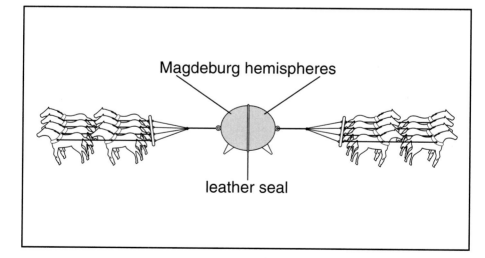

Two eight-horse teams could not pull the Magdeburg hemispheres apart.

FIGURE 18

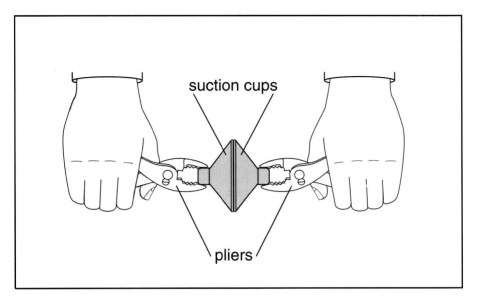

Two suction cups serve nicely in a small-scale Magdeburg hemispheres experiment.

with a 5-cm (2-in) diameter. You can buy suction cups in a hardware store. Remove any hooks that may be on the cups. Then wet the two suction cups with water. Put them firmly together. You will probably not be able to pull the cups apart with your fingers. You may have more success if you try to pull them apart with pliers, as shown in Figure 18. But even if you succeed, you must agree that air can exert powerful forces. This is particularly true if the air is pushing against a vacuum.

Experiment *4.6

SUCTION CUP AND CARD

To do this experiment you will need:

- ✔ an ADULT
- ✔ 2-in suction cup (from a hardware store)
- ✔ drill and small (2-mm or 1/16-in) bit
- ✔ playing card
- ✔ table

One of the suction cups you used as a Magdeburg hemisphere can be modified for this experiment. **ASK AN ADULT** to drill a small hole through the center of the suction cup (see Figure 19a).

Put a smooth playing card on a table. Place the suction cup with the hole in it on the playing card. Press down on the cup to push out some air from under the cup. Then place your finger firmly over the center hole, as shown in Figure 19b. Use your other fingers to grip the neck of the suction cup around the hole. You will find that you can lift the card off the table. What happens when you lift your finger to uncover the hole?

You could use this experiment as part of a science magic act. Show the audience that you can lift the card with the cup. Then invite someone to try it. Since that person does not know about the hole in the cup, he or she will not be able to lift the card. Perhaps you can convince the audience that you have magical powers.

FIGURE 19

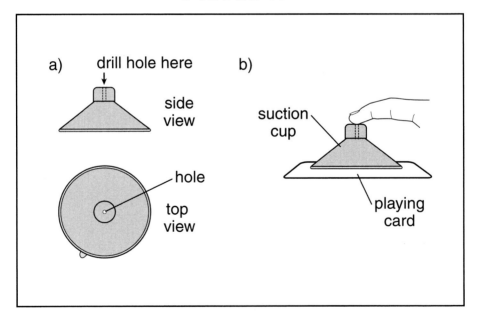

a) **ASK AN ADULT** to drill a small hole through the neck of a suction cup.

b) Place your finger over the hole in the suction cup. You will be able to lift a playing card with the cup!

And 'tis my faith that every flower
Enjoys the air it breathes.

(William Wordsworth)

5

MORE ABOUT AIR

We cannot live without air. Air contains the oxygen that our bodies need. The oxygen in air is also needed to make things burn. Without air, the gas and oil furnaces that heat our houses, schools, and other buildings will not work. Without air, the giant coal-, oil-, and gas-fired boilers that produce the steam to make electricity in many power plants will not work.

Swiftly moving air has its own strange properties. Moving air, as you will see, has less sideways pressure than still air. It is this property of moving air that makes an atomizer work and a baseball curve.

You will investigate air, lung air, moving air, and burning in the experiments that follow.

DID YOU KNOW. . .?

The lungs of an average adult man can hold a maximum of 5.3 L of air. During each breath in normal breathing, 500 ml (0.5 L) of air move into and out of the lungs. Normally, the lungs contain about 3.0 L after air is exhaled and 3.5 L after air is inhaled.

Experiment *5.1

CANDLE BURNING AND AIR

To do this experiment you will need:

- ✔ short candle (about 2.5 cm [1 in] tall) in short candleholder, or birthday candle supported by lump of clay
- ✔ an ADULT
- ✔ matches
- ✔ wide-mouthed glass jars of different volumes: 0.5L (1 pint), 1L (1qt), 2L (2qt), 4L (1 gal)
- ✔ stopwatch, or a watch or clock with a second hand

When a candle burns, the wax combines with oxygen in the air to form carbon dioxide and gaseous water (water vapor). Does the amount of air affect the time a candle will burn? You can find out by burning a candle under jars of different sizes.

Place a short candle in a small candle-holder, or support a birthday candle with a small lump of clay, as shown in Figure 20a. **ASK AN ADULT** to light the candle. When the candle wax has melted around the wick and is burning brightly, **ASK THE ADULT** to place a 1-L (1-qt), wide-mouthed jar over the burning candle (Figure 20b). Use a stopwatch, or a watch or clock with a second hand, to measure how long the candle burns inside a liter (quart) of air. How long did the candle continue to burn?

How long do you think the candle will burn in a 0.5-L (1-pint) jar? in a 2-L (2-qt) jar? in a 4-L (1-gal) jar?

ASK AN ADULT to help you test your predictions. **ASK THE ADULT** to light the candle and place the jars over the burning candle. Measure the time that the candle burns in these different volumes of air. How does the volume of air affect the time that a candle will burn?

FIGURE 20

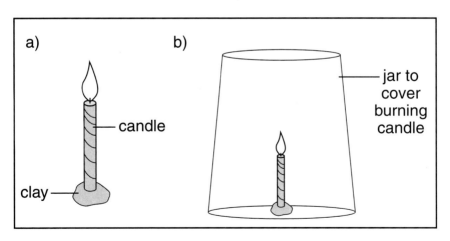

a) Support a candle with a small lump of clay.

b) How long will a candle burn in a 1-L (1-qt) jar?

Experiment *5.2

A BURNING CANDLE AND LUNG AIR

To do this experiment you will need:

- ✔ an ADULT
- ✔ sink, basin, or pail
- ✔ water
- ✔ 1-L (1-qt) wide-mouthed glass jar
- ✔ flexible drinking straw
- ✔ short candle (about 1 in tall) in short candleholder, or birthday candle supported by small lump of clay
- ✔ stopwatch, or a watch or clock with a second hand

In the last experiment, you saw that air is needed for a candle to burn. You also found that the candle's burn time depends on the amount of air available. Doubling the volume of air just about doubles the time the candle will burn.

How long do you think a candle will burn in air you exhale from your lungs? You can find out by collecting some lung air in a jar. To do that, fill a sink, basin, or pail with water. Place a 1-L (1-qt) wide-mouthed jar in the water and let it fill. Turn the jar upside down. Place the short end of a flexible drinking straw under the mouth of the jar. Then blow air from your lungs into the jar. The air will push the water out of the way.

Once you have filled the jar with lung air, keep the mouth of the air-filled jar underwater. **ASK AN ADULT** to light a short candle in a small candleholder or a birthday candle supported by a lump of clay. Then **ASK THE ADULT** to quickly place the jar of lung air over the burning candle while you measure the time that the candle burns in the air from your lungs. How long does the candle burn in one liter of lung air? Does it burn as long in lung air as it did in one liter of ordinary air? Can you explain your results?

Experiment *5.3

Moving Air

To do this experiment you will need:

- ✔ an ADULT
- ✔ string
- ✔ tape
- ✔ 2 balloons
- ✔ glass
- ✔ water
- ✔ sink
- ✔ scissors
- ✔ drinking straw
- ✔ Ping-Pong ball or Styrofoam ball
- ✔ funnel
- ✔ vacuum cleaner that will blow air or a hair dryer
- ✔ empty half-liter (pint-sized) glass bottle
- ✔ clay
- ✔ birthday candle
- ✔ newspaper

Moving air produces some strange effects. You will examine several of these effects in the experiments that follow.

Moving Air Between Balloons

Use string and tape to hang two balloons side by side, as shown in Figure 21. Leave about 10 cm (4 in) of space between the balloons. What happens when you

FIGURE 21

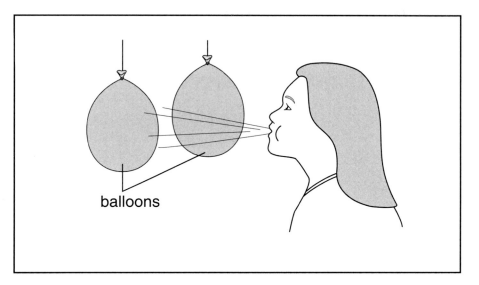

balloons

What happens when you blow air between two suspended balloons?

blow air between the balloons? Is the pressure greater in the moving air between the balloons or in the still air on their other sides? How can you tell? What happens when you blow along the side of just one balloon? Which way does it move?

A Drinking-Straw Atomizer

An atomizer is a device that produces a fine spray. It is often used for spraying perfume. You can use moving air to make a simple atomizer. Fill a glass with water and place it beside a sink. Use scissors to cut a drinking straw in half. Hold one half of the straw upright in the water. The top of the straw should be above the water in the glass. Using the other half of the straw, blow air across the top of the straw that is in the water (see Figure 22). A fine spray of water comes out of the upright straw. What must have happened to the pressure at the top of the upright straw?

FIGURE 22

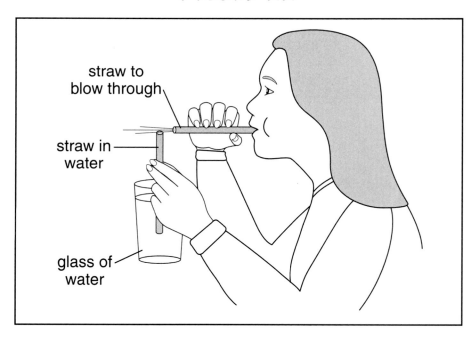

straw to blow through

straw in water

glass of water

A simple atomizer can be made from a drinking straw.

A Ping-Pong Ball That Defies Gravity

Place a Ping-Pong ball on a table. Put a funnel upside down over the ball, then blow into the funnel, as shown in Figure 23. You will find that you can lift the ball up with the funnel. The ball will remain in the funnel as long as you blow air over it. What must be true of the pressure above the ball where the air is moving? What holds the ball up? What happens when you stop blowing?

FIGURE 23

Ping-Pong ball inside funnel

As long as you blow into the funnel, the Ping-Pong ball will remain suspended.

You might like to do this experiment as a challenge to a friend or family member. Place an empty glass, a Ping-Pong ball, and a funnel on a table. The challenge is to lift the ball without touching it with your hand and place it in the empty glass.

A Floating Ping-Pong Ball

Find a vacuum cleaner that will blow as well as suck air. If you don't have such a vacuum cleaner, use a hair dryer. Produce an upward stream from the vacuum cleaner's or hair dryer's nozzle. Place a Ping-Pong ball in the air stream. You will find that you can make the ball float in the air stream like the one shown in Figure 24.

Blowing "Through" a Bottle

Place an empty half-liter (pint-sized) glass bottle on a table. Use a small lump of clay to support a birthday candle on one side of the bottle. **ASK AN ADULT** to light the candle. Put your head on the side of the bottle opposite the candle. Blow hard against the bottle. The candle will go out. Have you really blown air *through* the bottle?

FIGURE 24

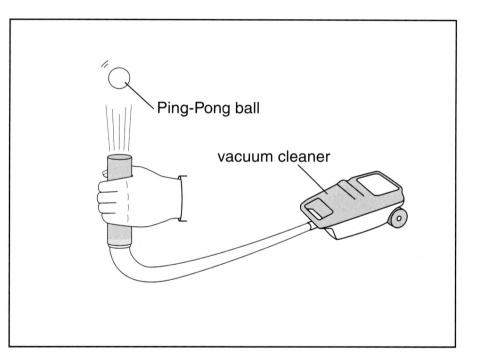

Ping-Pong ball

vacuum cleaner

A Ping-Pong ball will "float" in a fast-moving stream of air.

Throwing a Curve Ball

To make a ball curve, it must spin as it moves. The spinning ball drags air with it on one side. On the other side, its spin opposes the air, making the air move slower, as shown in Figure 25. You can make a Ping-Pong ball or a Styrofoam ball curve by launching it from a newspaper rolled up into a cone. As the ball rolls along the cone, it acquires a sideways spin that remains after it leaves the cone. Use your right hand to swing the cone from left to right across the front of your body, as shown in Figure 26. Which way does the ball curve?

Next, use your left hand to swing the cone with the ball from right to left across your body. Which way does the ball curve this time?

Moving Air and Pressure

In all six effects of moving air, the effect was caused by the low sideways pressure in moving air. The sideways pressure of moving air is less than the still air around it. Review each of the effects you looked at in Experiment 5.3. Can you see how the reduced pressure of moving air allowed the pressure of still air to move balloons and water; suspend, keep in place, or curve

FIGURE 25

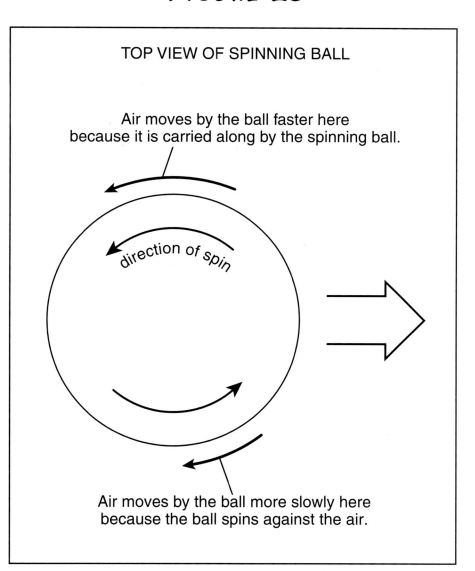

TOP VIEW OF SPINNING BALL

Air moves by the ball faster here
because it is carried along by the spinning ball.

direction of spin

Air moves by the ball more slowly here
because the ball spins against the air.

This drawing shows an overhead view of a spinning ball moving
from left to right. The ball is spinning counterclockwise (opposite
the direction that the hands of a clock move). Which way will the
ball curve?

FIGURE 26

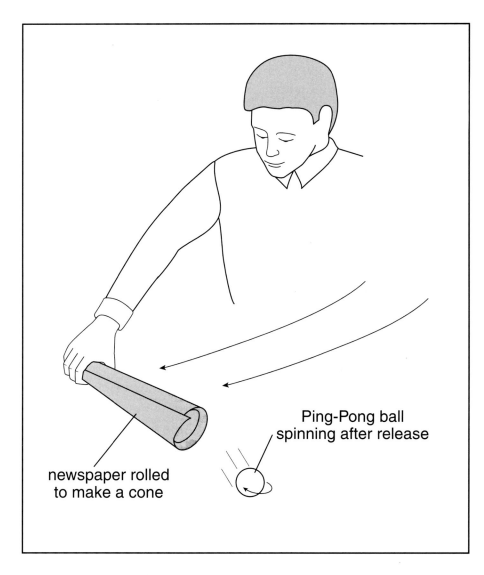

Ping-Pong ball
spinning after release

newspaper rolled
to make a cone

A ball can be made to spin by throwing it from a newspaper
rolled up into a cone.

Ping-Pong balls; and allow an air stream to flow around a bottle?

The same effect can be seen in sports. Baseball pitchers apply spin to the ball to make it curve or drop faster than normal. Tennis players "cut" the ball with their racquets to make it spin and curve both before and after it hits the court. Basketball players put spin on the ball when they shoot baskets to make the ball slow down when it hits the rim.

DID YOU KNOW. . .?

The ionosphere, which lies above the stratosphere and overlaps the mesosphere and thermosphere, contains ions (charged atoms). It is this layer that reflects radio and television waves that would otherwise escape into outer space.

FURTHER READING

Ardley, Neil. *Science Book of Air*. Orlando, Fla.: Harcourt Brace & Company, 1991.

Brandt, Keith. *Air*. Mahwah, N.J.: Troll Associates, 1985.

Gardner, Robert. *Science Experiments*. New York: Franklin Watts, 1988.

Jennings, Terry. *Air*. Danbury, Conn.: Children's Press, 1989.

Mebane, Robert, and Thomas Rybolt. *Air and Gases*. New York: Twenty-First Century Books, Inc., 1995.

Murphy, Bryan. *Experiment with Air*. Minneapolis, Minn.: The Lerner Group, 1991.

Prochnow, Dave, and Kathy Prochnow. *Why?: Experiments for the Young Scientist*. Blue Ridge Summit, Penn.: TAB Books, 1992.

Smith, Henry. *Amazing Air*. New York: William Morrow & Company, Inc., 1983.

Taylor, Barbara. *Air and Flying*. New York: Franklin Watts, 1991.

LIST OF MATERIALS

A
air pump
aluminum pie plates
aneroid barometer

B
ball
balloons
basin or sink
blacktop
bottle, plastic
bottles, 1-L, 2-L, 4-L
building with attic and
  basement
building with elevator
  and stairs

C
candle, birthday
clay
coffee can with cover
coin
cork

D
drill
drinking straws

F
freezer
funnel

G
glass tumbler
graduated cylinder

H
hair dryer
hammer
hill or mountain

J
jars

L
laboratory balance

M
masking tape
measuring cup
medicine cup

N
nail
newspaper

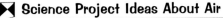

P
pail, small
paper clips
paper towel
pencil with eraser
petroleum jelly
Ping-Pong ball
plastic bag
playing card
pliers
pot holders or tongs

R
rubber band

S
scissors
seltzer tablets
soda can, empty
soup can, empty
spring balance

stove
string
Styrofoam ball
suction cups,
  5-cm

T
table
tape
thermometer
twisties

V
vaccuum cleaner that
  blows air

W
watch with second hand
weights

Y
yardstick

INDEX

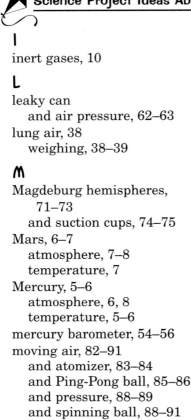